Freelance Freedom: The Essential Guide to Building a Successful Freelance Business

B. Vincent

Published by RWG Publishing, 2023.

While every precaution has been taken in the preparation of this book, the publisher assumes no responsibility for errors or omissions, or for damages resulting from the use of the information contained herein.

FREELANCE FREEDOM: THE ESSENTIAL GUIDE TO BUILDING A SUCCESSFUL FREELANCE BUSINESS

First edition. April 26, 2023.

Copyright © 2023 B. Vincent.

Written by B. Vincent.

Also by B. Vincent

Affiliate Marketing
Affiliate Marketing
Affiliate Marketing

Standalone
Business Employee Discipline
Affiliate Recruiting
Business Layoffs & Firings
Business and Entrepreneur Guide
Business Remote Workforce
Career Transition
Project Management
Precision Targeting
Professional Development
Strategic Planning
Content Marketing
Imminent List Building
Getting Past GateKeepers
Banner Ads
Bookkeeping
Bridge Pages
Business Acquisition

Business Bogging
Business Communication Course
Marketing Automation
Better Meetings
Business Conflict Resolution
Business Culture Course
Conversion Optimization
Creative Solutions
Employee Recruitment
Startup Capital
Employee Incentives
Employee Mentoring
Followership
Servant Leadership
Human Resources
Team Building
Freelancing
Funnel Building
Geo Targeting
Goal Setting
Immanent List Building
Lead Generation
Leadership Course
Leadership Transition
Leadership vs Management
LinkedIn Ads
LinkedIn Marketing
Messenger Marketing
New Management
Newsfeed Ads
Search Ads
Online Learning
Sales Webinars

Side Hustles
Split Testing
Twitter Timeline Advertising
Earning Additional Income Through Side Hustles: Begin Earning Money Immediately
Making a Living Through Blogging: Earn Money Working From Home
Create Bonuses for Affiliate Marketing: Your Success Is Encompassed by Your Bonuses
Internet Marketing Success: The Most Effective Traffic-Driving Strategies
JV Recruiting: Joint Ventures Partnerships and Affiliates
Secrets to List Building
Step-by-Step Facebook Marketing: Discover How To Create A Strategy That Will Help You Grow Your Business
Banner Advertising: Traffic Can Be Boosted by Banner Ads
Affiliate Marketing
Improve Your Marketing Strategy with Internet Marketing
Outsourcing Helps You Save Time and Money
Choosing the Right Content and Marketing for Social Media
Make Products That Will Sell
Launching a Product for Affiliate Marketing
Pinterest as a Marketing Tool
Banner Blitz: Mastering the Art of Advertising with Eye-Catching Banners
Beyond Commissions: Maximizing Affiliate Profits with Creative Bonus Strategies
Retargeting Mastery: Winning Sales with Online Strategies
Power Partnerships: Mastering the Art of Business Growth Through Partnership Recruiting
The List Advantage: Unlocking the Power of List Building for Marketing Success
Capital Catalyst: The Essential Guide to Raising Funds for Your Business

Mobile Mastery: The Ultimate Guide to Successful Mobile Marketing Campaigns

Crowdfunding Secrets: A Comprehensive Guide to Successfully Funding Your Next Project

Freelance Freedom: The Essential Guide to Building a Successful Freelance Business

Table of Contents

Chapter 1: Introduction - Why Freelance Freedom Matters 1

Chapter 2: Setting Yourself Up for Success - Establishing Your Freelance Business 5

Chapter 3: Finding Your Niche - How to Identify Your Freelance Specialization 7

Chapter 4: Crafting Your Brand - Developing Your Freelance Identity 9

Chapter 5: The Freelance Mindset - Cultivating a Successful Attitude 11

Chapter 6: Building Your Portfolio - Showcasing Your Best Work 13

Chapter 7: Setting Your Rates - Understanding Your Value and Pricing Strategies 15

Chapter 8: Building Your Network - Finding and Connecting with Clients 17

Chapter 9: Marketing Yourself - Getting Your Name Out There ... 19

Chapter 10: The Freelance Pitch - Mastering the Art of Selling Your Services 21

Chapter 11: The Contract Game - Understanding and Negotiating Freelance Contracts 23

Chapter 12: The Freelance Lifestyle - Balancing Work and Life 25

Chapter 13: Working with Clients - Building Strong Relationships 27

Chapter 14: Time Management for Freelancers - Tips and Techniques for Staying on Track 29

Chapter 15: Managing Your Finances - Understanding Taxes, Invoices, and Budgets 31

Chapter 16: Expanding Your Business - Scaling Up and Adding More Clients 33

Chapter 17: Dealing with Challenges - Overcoming Obstacles and Navigating Roadblocks 35

Chapter 18: The Future of Freelancing - Trends and Opportunities in the Gig Economy.. 37

Chapter 19: Staying Inspired - Finding Motivation and Staying Creative 39

Chapter 20: Conclusion - Celebrating Your Freelance Freedom ... 41

Chapter 1: Introduction - Why Freelance Freedom Matters

The nature of work is undergoing profound transformations at an accelerating rate, and the rise of the gig economy has presented people with exciting new opportunities to work for themselves and establish profitable freelance businesses. It should come as no surprise that an increasing number of people are choosing to work in a freelance capacity due to the independence and versatility that comes with doing so.

In this chapter, we will discuss the significance of having freedom to work independently, as well as the reasons why many people find this to be an appealing career option. We will also talk about the difficulties that come with freelancing as well as the advantages that make it something that is worth pursuing.

Freelancing gives people the opportunity to direct their own professional lives, which is the primary benefit of the arrangement. Freelancers, as opposed to employees of traditional companies, have the ability to pick and choose the projects they take on, as well as the customers and clients they collaborate with and the hours they put in. This flexibility is especially beneficial for people who need to juggle work with other obligations, such as taking care of members of their family or pursuing other interests in addition to their career.

In addition, individuals are able to pursue their individual passions and interests when they work as freelancers. For instance, if you enjoy writing and want to build a business for yourself, you might consider becoming a freelance copywriter or content creator. You might also consider becoming a freelance graphic designer if you have an eye for design and the ability to put it to use. Freelancing offers individuals the opportunity to turn their skills and interests into a successful career, and the possibilities are virtually limitless.

One more benefit of working for oneself as a freelancer is the opportunity to increase one's income. You have the ability to determine your own rates when you work as a freelancer, and you can take on as much work as you are able to complete. It is possible to build a successful business that provides a comfortable income if one is willing to put in the effort and is dedicated to the task at hand. The possibilities for expansion are virtually endless when one considers the fact that one can serve customers from all over the world.

However, being a freelancer does not come without its share of difficulties. The need for self-discipline and motivation is one of the most significant challenges that one must face. Because you do not have a traditional employer to monitor your performance and keep you accountable, it is up to you to organize your time and ensure that your work is completed in a timely manner. Freelancers are required to be proactive in finding clients and marketing their services, which can be time consuming and requires a certain level of business acumen. In addition, freelancers are responsible for generating their own income.

In spite of these obstacles, many people find that the freedom that comes with freelancing makes it an attractive career path to pursue. In the following chapters, we will discuss the essential steps for building a successful freelance business. These steps include determining your market niche, developing your brand, establishing your rates, and marketing your services. This guide will provide you with the knowledge and tools you need to succeed in your freelance business, regardless of whether you are just starting out or looking to take your business to the next level.

In conclusion, the introduction chapter provides an overview of the various factors that contribute to the allure of the freelancing lifestyle for a great number of people. Because of this, they are able to take charge of their professional lives, follow their interests, and potentially increase their income. Although freelancing presents its own unique set of difficulties, the numerous positive aspects make it an endeavor well worth pursuing. This guide will provide the steps that are necessary for building a successful freelancing business and achieving the freedom and flexibility that come along with it.

Chapter 2: Setting Yourself Up for Success - Establishing Your Freelance Business

You will need to establish some ground rules for your freelance business before you can get started on building it into a profitable venture. This chapter will cover the essential steps that need to be taken in order to set up your freelance business, such as researching relevant laws and designing an environment that encourages productivity in the workplace.

Choosing a legal structure for your freelancing venture should be the first thing you do when launching a new business. Some freelancers choose to run their businesses as sole proprietorships, while others opt to establish themselves as limited liability companies (LLCs) or corporations. Your personal circumstances as well as the kind of work that you do will influence the kind of legal structure that you go with. If you want to ensure that you are making the right decision for your company, it is essential to discuss the matter with a legal professional or a certified public accountant.

After you have decided on the appropriate legal structure for your company, it is time to develop a business plan. Your business plan should provide an overview of your objectives, ideal clientele, service offerings, and marketing approach. This plan will act as a road map for your company and assist you in maintaining your focus on the objectives you have set.

Creating an environment in your workspace that is conducive to productivity is yet another essential step in starting your own freelance business. This could be a room in your home that is specifically designated as an office, a shared office space, or even a coffee shop. It is essential to ensure that your workspace, in whatever form it may take, is cozy and devoid of any potential sources of distraction.

In addition to preparing a space for work, one of the most important things you can do is make investments in the equipment and materials your company will need to function properly. This might include a computer, some software, and various other supplies for an office. Think about what is necessary to ensure the smooth operation of your company, and then invest in that functionality right away.

Creating a website for your freelance business is another important step in getting it off the ground. Your website will act as your online presence and provide prospective customers with an opportunity to view examples of your work. It ought to include information about the services you provide, the rates you charge, and your portfolio. In order to establish yourself as an authority in your field, you might also want to include testimonials from satisfied customers and a blog.

To wrap things up, the final step in establishing your freelancing business is to get your finances in order. This includes setting up systems for invoicing and accounting, as well as keeping track of your business's expenses and opening a bank account specifically for the company. To ensure the financial success of your business from the very beginning, it is essential to maintain an organized and well-kept workspace and to keep detailed records.

In conclusion, establishing your freelancing business successfully requires careful deliberation and meticulous planning. You need to select a legal structure for your company, compose a business plan, set up a workspace that is conducive to productivity, make investments in the tools and resources that you will require, compose a website, and organize your finances. You will put yourself in a position to be successful and you will be well on your way to building a prosperous freelance business if you follow these steps.

Chapter 3: Finding Your Niche - How to Identify Your Freelance Specialization

Discovering your particular area of expertise is one of the most critical steps in establishing a profitable freelance business. You can establish yourself as an authority in a particular field if you choose to specialize in that field. This will enable you to attract customers who are looking for your one-of-a-kind skills and knowledge. In this chapter, we will discuss the steps that you can take to determine your area of expertise as a freelancer and carve out a specific space for yourself in the market.

The first thing you should do in order to find your niche is to evaluate the skills and interests you already possess. Spend some time reflecting on the kinds of work you enjoy doing and the kinds of skills you are particularly good at. Think about your education and previous work experience, as well as any hobbies or interests you have that you think you might be able to turn into a career as a freelancer. You can start to hone in on a specific area and concentrate on it by narrowing down your options after you have determined your capabilities and interests.

After you have a general idea of the kind of work you want to do, the next step is to conduct market research and determine the areas of the market where there is demand for your services. Researching job postings, online marketplaces, and trade publications can help you determine the kinds of freelance services that are currently in demand. This research will assist you in locating voids in the market that you, with your particular set of skills and experience, will be able to fill.

Understanding your ideal customer is another essential step in the process of finding your niche market. Think about your ideal customer and what they're looking for in a service provider. This will assist you in customizing your services and marketing efforts to attract the ideal customers for your business. You should also think about the competition in the specific niche that you have chosen, and devise strategies that will help you differentiate yourself from others and stand out in the market.

When you have found your particular area of specialization, the next step is to hone your abilities and become an expert in that field. This might involve enrolling in classes, going to conferences, or searching for mentors who can guide your professional development and help you hone your skills. You can establish yourself as a thought leader in your field and bring in more high-paying customers if you continue to educate yourself and grow professionally in that field.

Last but not least, it is essential to maintain a flexible mindset and be willing to make adjustments in response to shifting market conditions. It is important to keep an open mind and be willing to try new things and opportunities because the nature of your niche may shift over time. Maintain an awareness of the most recent developments in your industry, and be flexible enough in your approach to business to accommodate shifting conditions as they arise.

In a nutshell, determining your area of expertise is one of the most important steps in establishing a prosperous freelance business. You can find your unique niche in the market and position yourself for success by conducting an evaluation of your skills and interests, conducting research on the market, gaining an understanding of your target market, building your skills and expertise, and maintaining a flexible mindset.

Chapter 4: Crafting Your Brand - Developing Your Freelance Identity

Your company's brand is much more than its logo or website; rather, it is the very essence of the freelance business you run. It is the means by which you convey your value to customers and set yourself apart from the rivalry of other businesses. In this chapter, we will discuss the steps you can take to develop your freelance identity and craft a brand that resonates with your target market. These steps can be taken individually or in conjunction with one another.

Determining your one-of-a-kind value proposition should be the first thing you do when developing your brand. The value that you provide to customers is what separates you from the other businesses in the industry. Take into account not only your expertise, experience, and skills, but also your personality and the way you approach your work. What sets you apart from other freelancers working in the same field as you do? Make use of this information to craft a one-of-a-kind value proposition that effectively conveys the advantages of doing business with you.

After you have determined your value proposition, the next step is to develop a brand identity that is congruent with it. This includes aspects such as your company's logo and color scheme, as well as the design of your website. Your company's website, as well as your profiles on various social media platforms, as well as your email signature and business cards, should all have a unified and consistent presentation of your brand identity. Maintaining coherence across all of your marketing efforts and interactions with potential customers is critical to the success of your brand.

Developing a compelling brand message is another essential step in the process of developing your brand. This is the narrative that you share about your company, including who you are, what you do, and the motivation behind what you do. Your company's message ought to be understandable, succinct, and easy to recall; it should also reverberate with the people you're trying to reach. You can communicate your one-of-a-kind value proposition to potential customers by using your brand message, and you can also use it to establish an emotional connection with them.

Your brand consists of more than just the visual components and the messaging you use; it also includes the way you interact with customers. This includes the way in which you present yourself in meetings and other interactions, as well as your communication style and approach to providing excellent customer service. Be sure that your interactions are in line with the identity of your brand, and that you always present yourself in a way that is positive and professional.

Lastly, it is essential to monitor and keep up with the maintenance of your brand over time. This entails keeping abreast of the latest developments in your industry as well as the shifting requirements of your clientele and adapting your brand accordingly in order to maintain its relevance. It also means taking an active role in managing your online reputation and providing a response to the comments and reviews left by customers.

In conclusion, developing your personal brand is an important step in the process of establishing a prosperous freelance business. You can establish yourself as an authority in your field and attract the clients that your company needs by defining your unique value proposition, developing a consistent brand identity, creating a powerful brand message, and maintaining your brand over time. This will allow you to bring in the customers who are the best fit for your company.

Chapter 5: The Freelance Mindset - Cultivating a Successful Attitude

The lifestyle of a freelancer comes with a number of advantages, but in order to be successful, one must adopt a specific mentality. In this chapter, we will discuss the fundamental aspects that make up the freelancer's mindset, as well as the ways in which you can cultivate a positive and successful attitude to support your freelance business.

The mindset of a freelancer places a premium on self-discipline as one of the most essential components. As a freelancer, it is your responsibility to keep track of your time and ensure that your work is proceeding as planned. This calls for self-discipline as well as the ability to organize your responsibilities in a prioritized manner and maintain concentration on your objectives. Setting clear goals and deadlines, breaking down larger tasks into smaller, more manageable steps, and eliminating distractions during work hours are some of the strategies that can be utilized to cultivate greater levels of self-discipline.

A willingness to take risks and an openness to the unknown are two additional essential components of the mindset of a freelancer. Freelancing is fraught with inherent risk, and as you build your business, you might find yourself alternately swimming in work and starving for it. To maintain your resilience and adaptability in the face of shifting conditions, it can be helpful to cultivate a mindset that is willing to take calculated risks and is open to the possibility of uncertainty. This might require you to get out of your comfort zone, try new approaches to your work, and be willing to learn from your mistakes.

The mindset of a freelancer must include, in addition to self-discipline and a willingness to take risks, a positive and proactive attitude. This includes taking responsibility for your work and your career, maintaining a high level of motivation and engagement with your work, and being proactive in finding new customers and marketing your services. You can stay focused on your goals, overcome challenges, and strike a healthy balance between your work and your personal life if you keep a positive attitude.

The ability to keep a healthy work-life balance while also being able to effectively manage stress is another crucial component of the mindset of a freelancer. Working for yourself as a freelancer can be stressful; therefore, it is essential to find ways to manage stress and prevent burnout. This may involve establishing boundaries between work and personal life, taking breaks throughout the day, and participating in activities that are beneficial to one's health and well-being, such as working out, meditating, or engaging in hobbies.

In conclusion, adopting the mindset of a freelancer requires a dedication to continuous improvement in one's professional abilities. As a freelancer, it is your responsibility to keep up with the latest trends in your industry and continue to develop your skills in order to remain competitive. This might involve going to conferences, enrolling in classes, or searching for mentors in your industry who can guide your professional development.

In a nutshell, developing the mentality of a successful freelancer is absolutely necessary in order to establish a prosperous freelance business. Self-discipline, a willingness to take risks, a positive and proactive attitude, skills in stress management, and a commitment to ongoing learning and professional development are all necessities for this endeavor. You can put yourself in a position to be successful and build a freelance career that is both fulfilling and rewarding if you cultivate these elements of the freelance mindset.

Chapter 6: Building Your Portfolio - Showcasing Your Best Work

Your portfolio is one of the most important and valuable assets you have as a freelancer. Because it provides a visual representation of your skills and expertise, it can assist you in attracting new customers and securing new business. In this chapter, we will discuss the fundamentals of constructing a robust portfolio and exhibiting your finest work to prospective customers. This is an important step in the career development process.

Choosing your best work is the first thing you should do when putting together a portfolio. This may include examples of projects that you have finished for previous clients, projects that you have completed for yourself, or examples of work that you have completed as part of your education or training. It is important to choose work that not only showcases the kind of work you want to do more of in the future but also demonstrates your skills and expertise in the field that you have chosen.

After you have chosen the pieces of your portfolio that you are most proud of, the next step is to arrange them in a manner that is user-friendly for prospective customers. This could involve creating a website for your online portfolio or utilizing a platform such as Behance or Dribbble to display your work online. It is important that your portfolio be well-organized, have a visually appealing design, and be simple to navigate.

Creating a portfolio that is tailored to your target market is an additional crucial step in the process of building a strong portfolio. Think about the kinds of customers you want to bring in as well as the kinds of work they are most likely to be interested in. Check to see that your portfolio demonstrates your experience and skills in the aforementioned areas, and that it also caters to the requirements and interests of the audience you intend to reach.

In addition to providing examples of your previous work, your portfolio should also include a narrative that discusses your company and brand. This may entail incorporating your brand identity into the design of your portfolio or adding case studies and testimonials that showcase the results you've achieved for previous clients. Both of these options are excellent ways to demonstrate your success. Make the most of the opportunity presented by your portfolio to communicate your one-of-a-kind value proposition to prospective customers and to establish your brand identity in their eyes.

Last but not least, make sure that your portfolio is always up to date and that you add new pieces of work as you finish new projects. This will help to maintain the freshness and relevance of your portfolio, as well as demonstrate your ongoing growth and development as a freelancer.

To summarize, if you want to attract new customers and win new business as a freelancer, developing a robust portfolio is absolutely necessary. To accomplish this, you will need to choose the best of your work, arrange it in a way that makes it simple to navigate, modify it so that it is relevant to your target audience, and use it to tell a story about your company and your brand. You can establish yourself as an authority in your field and attract ideal customers to your company if you keep your portfolio up to date and highlight your best work. This will bring in more money for your company.

Chapter 7: Setting Your Rates - Understanding Your Value and Pricing Strategies

Figuring out how much they should charge for their services is one of the most difficult tasks facing freelancers. Even though it may be tempting to underprice yourself in order to bring in more customers, it is essential to comprehend the value that you bring to the table and charge an appropriate amount for your services. In this chapter, we will discuss the most important aspects of establishing your rates as a freelancer. These aspects include gaining an understanding of your value, developing pricing strategies, and engaging in negotiation with clients.

Understanding your value is the first thing you need to do before setting your rates. Consider your skills, expertise, experience, and the unique value you offer to clients. It is essential to price your services in accordance with the value that you bring to the table, rather than simply charging an amount that you believe customers will be willing to pay. This may require you to conduct research on the rates used in the industry as well as compare your skills and experience to those of others working in your field.

After gaining a broad understanding of your value, it is time to settle on a pricing strategy for your offering. Freelancers have a variety of options available to them in terms of pricing models, including hourly rates, rates based on projects, and value-based pricing. Although charging by the hour is the most common method, it is important to keep in mind that this structure is not always the most profitable or efficient. While value-based pricing may be more appropriate for high-value projects in which the end result is more important than the amount of time spent on the project, project-based rates may be more appropriate for smaller, less well-defined endeavors.

Being transparent with customers about your pricing structure and the returns they can anticipate on their investments is another essential component of setting your prices correctly. Think about drawing up a pricing guide that lays out your rates and describes what customers can anticipate receiving at each price point. Taking these steps will make it easier for you to manage client expectations and ensure that customers are not taken aback by the total cost of their project.

In addition to determining your prices, it is essential to negotiate with customers whenever the opportunity presents itself. This may entail having a conversation about the breadth of the project, articulating the client's precise expectations, and settling on a final price that is acceptable to both parties. During these negotiations, it is essential to be open and honest with one another in order to find a solution that satisfies the needs of both parties.

In conclusion, it is essential to be adaptable and ready to modify your pricing structure in accordance with the development of your company. As you gain more experience, hone new skills, or become an expert in a particular field, your rates might shift to reflect these changes. In order to ensure that you are pricing your services at a level that is comparable to other providers in your industry, it is essential to remain current on the rates that are being charged by other businesses and to adjust your prices accordingly.

To summarize, determining your rates as a freelancer requires an awareness of your value, the selection of an appropriate pricing strategy, honesty and openness with clients, the ability to negotiate when appropriate, and the maintenance of flexibility and adaptability as your company develops. You can put yourself in a position to be successful and build a thriving freelance business by basing your rates on the value you bring to your clients and employing a pricing strategy that is beneficial for both you and your clients.

Chapter 8: Building Your Network - Finding and Connecting with Clients

Building a solid network is absolutely necessary if you want to find new clients and expand your business if you work as a freelancer. In this chapter, we will discuss the fundamentals of building your network, which include locating potential customers, developing networking strategies, and fostering positive relationships with existing customers.

The first thing you need to do in order to construct your network is locate potential customers. Think about the kinds of customers you'd like to work with and the locations where you might find them. This may involve researching upcoming industry events and conferences, building relationships with other freelancers working in your field, and utilizing social media to connect with prospective customers. Rather than merely focusing on selling your services, it is critical to put your attention on developing relationships with potential customers and adding value to their lives.

Creating a robust online presence for yourself is an additional essential step in the process of building your network. It's possible that this will require you to create a profile on social media platforms such as LinkedIn, Twitter, and Instagram, in addition to a professional website that highlights your experience and expertise. Make use of these platforms to share your work, interact with potential customers, and display your expertise in the relevant field.

In addition to engaging in offline networking activities, such as going to industry events and gatherings, it is essential to do so in order to meet prospective customers in person. This may prove to be a fruitful opportunity for you to cultivate new relationships, gain insight into emerging patterns and possibilities, and establish yourself as an authority in your field. Be prepared to talk about who you are and the work that you do, and then follow up with potential clients after the event to continue the conversation and introduce yourself again.

Keeping the relationships you have with your customers and clients up to date is another essential component of building your network. This includes maintaining communication with previous customers, delivering outstanding customer service, and actively seeking opportunities for repeat business and referrals from satisfied customers. You might want to think about sending regular updates and newsletters to previous customers, as well as asking for feedback on your work and offering exceptional service that goes above and beyond what they anticipate.

In conclusion, it is essential to take initiative when searching for new business partners and opportunities. This may include making a pitch for your services to prospective customers, responding to job postings, and looking for opportunities to work with other freelancers or businesses. Don't be afraid to explore new opportunities that are a good fit for your skills and experience, and don't let fear stop you from thinking creatively.

In conclusion, expanding your professional network is one of the most important aspects of growing your freelance business. In order to accomplish this, it is necessary to locate prospective customers, construct a solid online presence, participate in trade shows and conventions, continue to build and strengthen relationships with existing customers, and actively seek out new business opportunities. You can establish yourself as an authority in your field and attract the clients you need to run a successful business by putting your attention toward developing relationships with potential customers and providing value to those customers.

Chapter 9: Marketing Yourself - Getting Your Name Out There

When you're a freelancer, marketing yourself is absolutely necessary for establishing your brand and bringing in new customers. In this chapter, we will discuss the most important aspects of marketing yourself as a freelancer. These aspects include developing a marketing plan, making use of social media, and coming up with a content strategy.

Developing a marketing plan is the initial step in the process of marketing yourself. This should include having a solid comprehension of your target market, the services you provide, as well as the one-of-a-kind value proposition you bring to the table. Consider utilizing content marketing, social media marketing, and email marketing, among other channels and strategies, in order to communicate with prospective customers. It is essential to devise a strategy that can be carried out, is based on facts, and is in keeping with the financial constraints and objectives of your company.

When you're trying to market yourself as a freelancer, social media is one of the most important tools you can use. Consider which platforms are the most pertinent to your target audience, and then create profiles for those platforms that reflect the identity of your brand and the value proposition you offer. Make use of various social media platforms to disseminate your work, interact with prospective customers, and illustrate your level of expertise within your industry. Think about using paid advertising so that you can reach a larger audience and target prospective customers based on their demographics and the things that they are interested in.

Creating a content strategy is an additional essential part of marketing yourself as a product or service. Creating blog posts, articles, or videos that highlight your expertise and provide value to prospective customers can be one way to go about accomplishing this goal. It is essential to produce content that is pertinent to your target audience and that demonstrates your distinct value proposition in a way that stands out from the competition. You can build trust with potential customers and establish yourself as an expert in your field by using the content you create.

In addition to producing content, it is essential to look for opportunities to contribute as a guest blogger or to speak at events related to your industry. Reaching new audiences and establishing yourself as an authority in your field can be accomplished through the use of this helpful method. You could try submitting guest posts to blogs or websites that are pertinent to your field, or you could look for opportunities to speak at conferences or meetups.

In conclusion, it is essential to keep a record of your marketing activities and to evaluate the outcomes. This may involve using analytics tools to track website traffic and engagement on social media, as well as monitoring the effectiveness of your email marketing campaigns and other marketing efforts. In addition, this may involve tracking the number of subscribers to your mailing list. Make use of this information to improve your marketing plan and make any necessary adjustments to your strategy so that you can accomplish your business goals.

To summarize, marketing yourself as a freelancer requires having a firm grasp on your ideal clientele, having an established marketing strategy, putting an emphasis on the production of valuable content, and interacting with prospective customers via social media and other platforms. You can put yourself in a position to be successful and build a prosperous freelancing business by utilizing these strategies and measuring the results of your efforts.

Chapter 10: The Freelance Pitch - Mastering the Art of Selling Your Services

As a freelancer, it is imperative that you become skilled in the art of the pitch in order to acquire new customers and expand your business. In this chapter, we will discuss the most important aspects of a successful freelance pitch. These aspects include gaining an understanding of the needs of your client, developing an engaging pitch, and securing the deal.

Understanding the requirements of your client is the first step in developing a successful pitch for your freelance work. Conduct research on the customer and their company, then determine the difficulties they are experiencing as well as the objectives they wish to accomplish. This will allow you to tailor your pitch to their specific requirements and demonstrate your value as a potential solution to the issues they are facing.

To create a compelling presentation, you must concentrate on the requirements of the client and the ways in which you can assist them in accomplishing their objectives. Start off with a convincing introduction that demonstrates your credibility and your level of expertise in the subject matter. Explain in detail the services you provide and the ways in which they can benefit the customer, providing concrete illustrations and use cases to back up your claims about your worth. Take into account any possible reservations that the customer may have, and then present them with a crystal-clear call to action that persuades them to move forward with the process.

When presenting your services to a potential client, it is essential to not only develop an engaging pitch, but also to exude self-assurance and a friendly demeanor. You should rehearse your presentation and be ready to answer any questions that the client might have. Maintain a positive and enthusiastic attitude throughout the entirety of the presentation, and make sure to use language that is straightforward and simple to grasp.

To successfully close the deal, it is necessary to place primary emphasis on constructing trust and achieving a comprehensive comprehension of the parameters of the project. Maintain open and honest communication with the client regarding your pricing, the extent of the project, and the timeframe for its completion. Be willing to negotiate on terms that are beneficial to both parties and address any concerns that the customer may have. After the transaction has been finalized, it is important to check in with the client to ascertain whether or not they are pleased with the work performed and to look for additional opportunities for repeat business and referrals.

Last but not least, it's essential to keep honing your pitch and adjusting it to meet the requirements of a variety of clientele and business sectors. Depending on the type of client you're targeting with your presentation, this may necessitate developing multiple iterations of your pitch. Alternatively, you may choose to test out a variety of approaches and methods to determine which one is most successful.

In conclusion, mastering the art of the freelance pitch necessitates concentrating on the requirements of the client, delivering a presentation that is compelling and self-assured, having a crystal clear understanding of the parameters of the project, and committing to continuous improvement and adjustment. If you are able to master the pitch, you will be able to establish yourself as an authority in your field, which will allow you to win new clients and grow your freelance business.

Chapter 11: The Contract Game - Understanding and Negotiating Freelance Contracts

When you work as a freelancer, one of the most important things you can do to build your business and protect your interests is to negotiate contracts. In this chapter, we will discuss the fundamentals of understanding freelance contracts and negotiating payment terms. These fundamentals include common contract terms, the protection of your intellectual property, and the negotiation of payment terms.

Understanding the common terms and clauses that are typically included in a freelance contract is the first step in the negotiation process for such a contract. The terms of payment, the scope of the project, the timelines, and any termination clauses may be included in this. It is essential to give contracts a thorough read through and, if necessary, to consult an attorney in order to ensure that you fully comprehend both the terms of the agreement as well as its repercussions.

The negotiation of freelance contracts involves a number of important aspects, one of which is the protection of one's intellectual property. Inclusion of clauses that specify who owns the rights to the work, how it can be used, and how any intellectual property disputes will be resolved may be required to accomplish this goal. To ensure that your interests are protected and that your contract is in alignment with your business goals, you may want to consider consulting with a lawyer.

One of the most important aspects of negotiating a freelance contract is determining how payments will be made. This may involve negotiating a deposit up front, setting up a payment schedule, or establishing penalties for late payments. It is essential to communicate your payment expectations to clients in a straightforward and open manner, and to look for payment terms that are satisfactory to both parties involved.

In addition to these essential components, it is essential to maintain an open and honest line of communication with clients throughout the entirety of the negotiation process. Be ready to address any concerns or objections that the customer may have, and be willing to negotiate terms that are beneficial to both parties. If you want to reduce the likelihood of misunderstandings leading to legal battles in the future, you might want to think about including a clause in the contract that outlines the process by which any disagreements will be settled.

Last but not least, it is critical to ensure that complete and accurate records of all agreements and contracts are maintained. This may involve utilizing software or other tools to manage contracts and agreements, in addition to maintaining open communication with customers throughout the entirety of the project.

To summarize, being able to comprehend and successfully negotiate freelance contracts calls for a concentration on common contract terms, the protection of your intellectual property, the negotiation of payment terms, and the maintenance of clear communication with clients throughout the process. You can create a successful freelancing business for yourself and position yourself for long-term success by negotiating contracts that safeguard your interests and are in line with the goals you have set for your company.

Chapter 12: The Freelance Lifestyle - Balancing Work and Life

It is essential for a freelancer to strike a healthy balance between their work and personal lives in order to prevent burnout and ensure continued success over the long term. In this chapter, we'll discuss the essential components of striking a healthy work-life balance as a freelancer, such as establishing clear boundaries, developing efficient time management skills, and making self-care a top priority.

Establishing distinct limits between one's professional and personal lives is the first thing that needs to be done in order to achieve a healthy work-life balance. This may involve establishing clear expectations regarding communication and availability, as well as setting specific work hours and communicating them to clients and coworkers. It is essential to make time for personal pursuits and relationships that are not related to one's work and to refrain from overcommitting oneself and working an excessive amount of hours.

Another essential component of successfully juggling work and life as a freelancer is practicing efficient time management. Managing your schedule and ensuring that you are making the most of the time you have available may require the utilization of time management tools such as calendars and software for tracking time. To boost your productivity and protect yourself from mental exhaustion, you might want to give the Pomodoro Technique a shot. This time-management system divides your workday into 25-minute chunks followed by brief breaks.

In order to keep a healthy work-life balance, it is also essential to place a priority on self-care. This might entail taking short breaks throughout the day, engaging in physical activity on a consistent basis, and engaging in activities that help reduce stress, such as yoga or meditation. Spending time with loved ones, pursuing hobbies, and traveling are examples of activities that should be prioritized outside of the workplace. It is also important to find activities that help you recharge your batteries.

As a last point of consideration, it is essential for a freelancer to actively seek out support and community. This could entail joining professional organizations or networking groups, going to events and conferences related to the industry, or making connections with other freelancers through social media or online communities. You can prevent feelings of isolation or exhaustion at work by cultivating a support network and surrounding yourself with other professionals who share your values. This will allow you to continue to feel motivated and inspired in your work.

To summarize, maintaining a healthy work-life balance as a freelancer requires establishing distinct boundaries, practicing efficient time management, making self-care a top priority, and actively seeking out support and community. As a freelancer, you can set yourself up for long-term success and a sense of fulfillment if you make caring for your health a priority and strike a good balance between your work and personal life.

Chapter 13: Working with Clients - Building Strong Relationships

Building solid relationships with customers is one of the most important things you can do as a freelancer if you want to see your business grow and be successful over the long term. In this chapter, we will discuss the most important aspects of working with clients, such as the importance of providing excellent customer service, effectively communicating with clients, and managing their expectations.

The ability to communicate clearly and effectively is the first step in developing solid relationships with customers. This may involve establishing clear communication channels, establishing expectations regarding response times, and ensuring that all communications are carried out with language that is both clear and concise. It is essential to pay attention to the wants and worries of your customer and to address any questions or problems in a prompt and expert manner whenever they come up.

Another crucial component of working with clients is effectively managing their expectations. This may involve communicating any changes or updates as they come up, as well as establishing clear expectations regarding the timeline of the project, the deliverables, and the scope of the work. You might want to think about using project management tools to help you keep track of deadlines and deliverables. Additionally, you might want to ask clients for feedback on a regular basis to ensure that you are living up to their expectations.

Building strong relationships with customers requires a number of things, one of which is providing exceptional customer service. This may involve going above and beyond to ensure that clients are satisfied with the work you have done for them, being responsive and available throughout the duration of the project, and looking for opportunities for repeat business and referrals. To demonstrate to your customers that you appreciate their business and are dedicated to their prosperity, you might want to think about sending thank-you notes or engaging in other forms of public demonstrations of gratitude.

In addition to these essential components, it is essential to be proactive in identifying and resolving any potential problems or difficulties that may crop up during the course of the project. These issues and difficulties may arise at any time. This may involve actively seeking the client's feedback and promptly addressing any concerns, being transparent about any issues that may have an impact on the project timeline or deliverables, and demonstrating a willingness to make adjustments or changes in order to guarantee that the client's requirements are satisfied.

In conclusion, it is essential to conduct yourself in a manner that is both professional and upbeat whenever you are interacting with customers. This may involve being responsive and courteous to the client, respecting the client's time as well as their requirements, and being willing to adapt and adjust as required to meet the client's expectations.

To summarize, cultivating strong relationships with customers requires effective communication, the management of expectations, the provision of exceptional customer service, and the demonstration of proactivity in the identification and resolution of potential problems or difficulties. You can establish yourself as a trusted partner in the success of your clients and position yourself for long-term success as a freelancer if you put an emphasis on relationship building and providing value to your clients.

Chapter 14: Time Management for Freelancers - Tips and Techniques for Staying on Track

Your ability to maximize your productivity and accomplish your professional objectives as a freelancer relies heavily on your ability to effectively manage your time. Setting priorities, developing a schedule, and avoiding distractions are three of the most important aspects of effective time management for freelancers, all of which will be discussed in this chapter.

Establishing distinct priorities for each aspect of your work is the first step in efficient time management. It's possible that this will require making a list of tasks and sorting them in order of importance and how quickly they need to be completed. To prioritize your work and ensure that you are as productive as possible, you should think about applying the 80/20 rule. This principle dictates that you should concentrate your efforts on the 20% of activities that are responsible for producing 80% of the results.

Another essential component of effective time management for freelancers is the development of a schedule. This may involve establishing specific work hours and allocating specific blocks of time to particular activities, projects, and responsibilities. To effectively manage your time and ensure that you are allocating it in the most productive way possible, you should think about using a calendar or another scheduling tool. If you want to avoid burnout and keep your energy levels up, it is essential to construct your schedule in a way that allows for regular breaks and downtime.

A crucial component of efficient time management is eliminating distractions whenever possible. This may entail establishing boundaries around your work environment, such as turning off notifications on your phone or closing your email inbox while you are working on something that requires your full attention. If you want to get rid of distractions and stay focused on your work, you should think about using tools like software that tracks time or blockers for websites.

In addition to these essential components, it is critical to demonstrate a willingness to modify and adapt your strategies for time management in response to changing circumstances. This may involve trying out a variety of strategies to determine which ones work best for you, or it may entail looking for support from coaches or mentors who can assist you in maintaining your current course of action.

Last but not least, one of the most important aspects of efficient time management is making one's own health and well-being a top priority. This might entail taking short breaks throughout the day, engaging in physical activity on a consistent basis, and engaging in activities that help reduce stress, such as yoga or meditation. You can set yourself up for long-term success as a freelancer by putting your health first and ensuring that you have a good balance between your work life and your personal life.

In conclusion, in order to effectively manage one's time as a freelancer, one must establish priorities, devise a schedule, steer clear of distractions, maintain a flexible mindset, and put self-care first. As a freelancer, you can position yourself for long-term success and a sense of fulfillment by concentrating on ways to increase your productivity and strike a healthy balance between your work and personal life.

Chapter 15: Managing Your Finances - Understanding Taxes, Invoices, and Budgets

When you're self-employed, one of the most important things you can do to ensure the success of your business and the achievement of your financial objectives is to practice good financial management. In this chapter, we will discuss the most important aspects of managing your finances as a freelancer, such as being aware of your tax obligations, developing and distributing invoices, and developing and adhering to a spending plan.

Understanding the tax obligations you have as a freelancer is the first step in effectively managing your personal finances. This may require conducting research on the applicable tax laws in your nation or region, as well as consulting an accountant or other tax professional for guidance. To simplify the process of filing your taxes, you should think about setting aside some of your income specifically to cover the cost of taxes, and you should also keep meticulous records of your income and expenses.

Managing your finances as a freelancer also requires you to create and send out invoices. This is an essential part of the process. Creating invoices with a professional appearance and including all of the necessary information, such as the scope of the project, payment terms, and your contact information, may require the use of software specifically designed for billing purposes or pre-designed templates. It is essential to promptly follow up on any invoices that are past due and to be transparent with clients about the payment expectations you have set for yourself.

When it comes to managing your finances as a freelancer, one of the most important things you can do is create a budget and stick to it. The use of a budgeting tool or a spreadsheet to keep track of your income and expenditures and the establishment of financial goals for your company are both potential steps in this process. You should give some thought to setting aside money not only for the costs associated with running your business, such as buying equipment and software, but also for your personal costs, such as rent and food. Be flexible and willing to make changes to your spending plan in order to meet your objectives and stay on track financially.

In addition to these essential components, it is critical to remain organized at all times and to maintain accurate records of all financial dealings. This may require you to manage your finances with the assistance of accounting software or other tools, in addition to keeping accurate and detailed records of your income and expenditures.

Finally, you should think about getting support and guidance from people who work in the financial industry or from other freelancers. This could entail joining professional organizations or networking groups, going to events and conferences related to the industry, or making connections with other freelancers through social media or online communities. You can keep yourself motivated and inspired in your work and succeed in achieving your financial goals if you construct a support system and surround yourself with other professionals who have similar values and perspectives.

In conclusion, if you want to successfully manage your finances as a freelancer, you need to devote your attention to learning about taxes, developing and distributing invoices, developing a budget and sticking to it, maintaining organization, and getting support and advice when you need it. You can set yourself up for long-term success as a freelancer if you make good financial management a priority and follow established best practices in the field.

Chapter 16: Expanding Your Business - Scaling Up and Adding More Clients

As a freelancer, one of the most important things you can do to move closer to achieving your goals and increasing your income is to grow your business and take on additional clients. In this chapter, we will discuss the essential components of expanding your company, such as scaling up your operations, increasing the number of customers you serve, and effectively managing the growth of your business.

The first thing you need to do in order to grow your company is to beef up your operations so that you can take on more customers and projects. In order to accomplish this goal, you may need to hire additional team members or contract out a portion of your work to other freelancers. You should think about using project management tools to manage your workflow and streamline your operations. Additionally, you should be willing to delegate tasks as necessary to ensure that you are able to handle an increased workload.

Increasing the size of your customer base is another crucial component of growing your business. This may involve networking with prospective customers, utilizing social media and online communities in order to reach a larger audience, and utilizing marketing strategies such as email marketing and content marketing in order to attract new customers. It is essential to be pro-active in the pursuit of new business opportunities, as well as to build solid relationships with one's existing customers, in order to increase the likelihood that these customers will continue to do business with one over the course of time.

When it comes to expanding your business as a freelancer, one of the most important things you can do is effectively manage growth. This may involve establishing crystal clear goals and benchmarks for growth, keeping track of your progress over time, and being willing to adapt and adjust your strategies as necessary in order to achieve your goals. Think about enlisting the guidance and assistance of a mentor or a business coach to assist you in navigating the challenges associated with growth and achieving the goals you have set for your company.

As a final point of consideration, it is essential to emphasize quality and excellent service to customers even as you grow your company. This may entail investing in training and development for yourself and other members of your team, soliciting feedback from customers as a means of enhancing your services, and placing a high priority on the level of satisfaction experienced by your clientele as a vital component of your overall business strategy.

To summarize, growing your business as a freelancer requires you to prioritize scaling up your operations, increasing the number of clients you work with, effectively managing your growth, and maintaining a focus on quality and customer service. As a freelancer, you can position yourself for long-term success and realize your business goals by adopting best practices for expanding your business and building a solid foundation for growth. In doing so, you can position yourself for long-term success and achieve your business goals.

Chapter 17: Dealing with Challenges - Overcoming Obstacles and Navigating Roadblocks

As a freelancer, you will inevitably come up against a variety of challenges and obstacles. It is important to develop strategies for effectively overcoming challenges and navigating roadblocks, whether it be dealing with difficult clients, facing financial struggles, or managing unexpected setbacks. It is also important to develop strategies for effectively navigating roadblocks. In this chapter, we'll discuss some of the most important aspects of dealing with challenges as a freelancer, such as learning how to manage stress, finding support, and building resilience.

Having an effective stress management strategy in place is the first step in overcoming challenges. This could involve engaging in activities that help reduce stress, such as meditation, physical exercise, or yoga. It could also involve prioritizing self-care and taking breaks throughout the day. You should give some thought to establishing boundaries around your working environment and being proactive in identifying and dealing with potential sources of stress before they become overwhelming.

Seeking support is another important step in the process of overcoming challenges when working as a freelancer. This may involve seeking advice and direction from mentors, coaches, or other professionals, in addition to seeking support from friends and family members. It is a good idea to join professional organizations or networking groups so that you can connect with other independent contractors and build a support system that can assist you in navigating the challenges of working as a freelancer.

Building up your resilience is another important skill to have as a freelancer in order to deal with the challenges you face. This may involve adopting a growth mindset and viewing setbacks as opportunities for learning and growth. It also may involve being willing to adapt and adjust your strategies as necessary to overcome obstacles. You should think about actively seeking out opportunities for training and development so that you can build new skills and capabilities. At the same time, you should focus on constructing a solid foundation of skills and expertise so that you can confidently navigate challenges.

In conclusion, it is essential to keep a positive and upbeat attitude throughout all of your interactions with customers and coworkers. This may involve rethinking obstacles as chances for personal development and concentrating on finding solutions rather than identifying problems. You should think about soliciting feedback from customers and coworkers in order to identify areas for improvement and to proactively address any concerns or problems that may arise.

In conclusion, if you want to be successful as a freelancer, you need to focus on learning how to manage stress, finding support, developing resilience, and keeping a positive and optimistic attitude at all times. You can position yourself for long-term success and fulfillment as a freelancer if you take steps to overcome challenges and effectively navigate roadblocks. By adopting strategies for overcoming challenges and effectively navigating roadblocks.

Chapter 18: The Future of Freelancing - Trends and Opportunities in the Gig Economy

Freelancing is becoming an increasingly popular and viable career option for professionals working in a wide variety of fields thanks to the ongoing expansion and development of the gig economy. This chapter will focus on the major developments and opportunities occurring within the gig economy, as well as how these factors are influencing the future of the independent work sector.

The rise of remote work and the ever-increasing value of digital skills are two important developments that are driving the gig economy. Freelancers with expertise in fields such as digital marketing, web design, and software development are in high demand as an increasing number of businesses are moving toward remote work arrangements. This pattern is likely to continue into the foreseeable future as companies search for workforce solutions that are both flexible and economical to meet their requirements.

One more significant movement is the expansion of the gig economy in emerging markets. This is because an increasing number of people in developing nations are turning to freelancing as a means of earning an income. This trend is being driven by factors such as rising internet access and the growing availability of digital payment platforms, both of which are making it simpler than ever before for freelancers to connect with clients and receive payment for their work. These are the factors that are driving this trend.

As businesses rely more and more on freelancers to provide specialized skills and expertise, more and more opportunities are opening up in the freelancing and gig economy. This pattern is especially noticeable in fields such as artificial intelligence, data analysis, and digital marketing, all of which require specialized skills and knowledge from businesses, which may not be readily available within the company itself.

The future of freelancing is also being shaped by technology, which is resulting in the development of new tools and platforms that can assist freelancers in managing their work and connecting with clients. Freelancers' work processes can be streamlined and their productivity can be improved, for instance, with the help of project management tools, collaboration platforms, and chatbots powered by artificial intelligence (AI).

In addition to these trends and opportunities, the future of freelancing is likely to be shaped by broader economic and social shifts, such as changes in the global labor market and evolving attitudes towards work-life balance and career fulfillment. In other words, the future of freelancing will be determined not only by these trends and opportunities, but also by broader economic and social shifts.

In a nutshell, the future of freelancing will be influenced by a wide variety of trends and opportunities, such as the increase in popularity of working from home, the expansion of the gig economy into developing countries, and the growing significance of possessing strong digital skills. Freelancers can position themselves for long-term success in the ever-changing gig economy by keeping abreast of these trends, adopting best practices for managing their work, and maintaining connections with clients.

Chapter 19: Staying Inspired - Finding Motivation and Staying Creative

Being able to maintain a high level of productivity and creativity in your work as a freelancer requires a high level of inspiration and motivation on a consistent basis. Finding motivation, maintaining creativity, and warding off burnout are three of the most important aspects of staying inspired while working as a freelancer, all of which will be discussed in this chapter.

Discovering what motivates you and pushing you toward your objectives is the first thing you need to do as a freelancer if you want to keep your inspiration levels high. This may involve establishing goals for your work that are specific and attainable, such as a certain number of clients or projects that are finished each month, and tracking your progress towards these goals. Think about connecting with peers and mentors who can offer advice and support as well as people whose experiences can serve as a source of inspiration, whether they be successful freelancers or entrepreneurs.

As a freelancer, maintaining your creativity is equally important to maintaining your inspiration. This may involve cultivating a creative mindset by engaging in activities such as taking breaks to refuel your creative energy, experimenting with new methods and tools, and seeking out feedback from customers and coworkers to improve your work. It is important to remain current on the most recent tendencies and methods in your field, so you should think about taking part in professional development opportunities or attending conferences and events.

As a freelancer, one of the most important things you can do to keep yourself inspired is to avoid burnout. This may involve establishing boundaries concerning your work hours and schedule, placing a high priority on self-care and wellness, and being willing to take breaks and step away from your work when it is necessary to do so. If you want to maintain your energy levels and keep your batteries charged up, you should give some thought to adopting stress-reducing activities such as exercising, meditating, or spending time in nature.

As a last point of consideration, it is essential for a freelancer to maintain a curious and open mind, as well as to actively seek out new opportunities for growth and challenges. This could mean taking on new clients or projects that are beyond your current level of expertise, or it could mean reaching out to other independent contractors or industry professionals in an effort to form working partnerships. You can keep a sense of wonder and excitement in your work, which will help you stay inspired and motivated over the long term. All you have to do is remain curious and open to new experiences.

In conclusion, if you want to remain inspired while working as a freelancer, you need to place an emphasis on finding motivation, maintaining creativity, avoiding burnout, and maintaining a curious and open mind. As a freelancer, you can set yourself up for long-term success and a sense of fulfillment by implementing best practices that help you keep your energy and creativity levels high.

Chapter 20: Conclusion - Celebrating Your Freelance Freedom

You should be armed with the knowledge and strategies required to build a successful freelance business and accomplish your goals as a freelancer as you near the conclusion of this guide. Congratulations on taking this significant action towards realizing your goals and establishing a foundation for a life of freedom as a freelancer!

We've covered a lot of ground throughout this guide, including the most important aspects of building a successful freelance business, such as locating your market niche and developing your brand, as well as managing your finances and growing your business. In addition to this, we have discussed methods for overcoming obstacles, maintaining inspiration, and successfully navigating the ever-changing gig economy.

You have the independence to choose your own path, follow your interests, and construct a business that is perfectly suited to your particular set of abilities, pursuits, and objectives when you work as a freelancer. This freedom is energizing and exhilarating in equal measure, but it also brings with it a significant amount of responsibility and requires a lot of hard work.

Take some time to think back on your journey and give yourself some credit for the things you've accomplished as you celebrate becoming a freelancer. You should give some thought to revising the objectives of your company and committing to a path of continuous growth and improvement. Make connections with other freelancers and professionals working in your field, and don't be afraid to talk about the lessons you've learned or the observations you've made.

It is important to keep in mind that achieving success as a freelancer is not only about achieving financial goals or building a successful business. It is also about discovering fulfillment and satisfaction in your work, as well as making a positive impact on the world. You have the potential to accomplish great things and make your mark as a successful freelancer if you remain true to your values and purpose and if you embrace the opportunities and challenges that come with the lifestyle of a freelancer.

In conclusion, the road to independence as a freelancer is not always an easy one, but the destination is always well worth the effort. You can build a successful and fulfilling career as a freelancer by putting in a lot of effort, being determined, and committing to ongoing learning and growth. If you do this, you can realize your dreams of having more freedom in your freelance work.

Also by B. Vincent

Affiliate Marketing
Affiliate Marketing
Affiliate Marketing

Standalone
Business Employee Discipline
Affiliate Recruiting
Business Layoffs & Firings
Business and Entrepreneur Guide
Business Remote Workforce
Career Transition
Project Management
Precision Targeting
Professional Development
Strategic Planning
Content Marketing
Imminent List Building
Getting Past GateKeepers
Banner Ads
Bookkeeping
Bridge Pages
Business Acquisition

Business Bogging
Business Communication Course
Marketing Automation
Better Meetings
Business Conflict Resolution
Business Culture Course
Conversion Optimization
Creative Solutions
Employee Recruitment
Startup Capital
Employee Incentives
Employee Mentoring
Followership
Servant Leadership
Human Resources
Team Building
Freelancing
Funnel Building
Geo Targeting
Goal Setting
Immanent List Building
Lead Generation
Leadership Course
Leadership Transition
Leadership vs Management
LinkedIn Ads
LinkedIn Marketing
Messenger Marketing
New Management
Newsfeed Ads
Search Ads
Online Learning
Sales Webinars

Side Hustles
Split Testing
Twitter Timeline Advertising
Earning Additional Income Through Side Hustles: Begin Earning Money Immediately
Making a Living Through Blogging: Earn Money Working From Home
Create Bonuses for Affiliate Marketing: Your Success Is Encompassed by Your Bonuses
Internet Marketing Success: The Most Effective Traffic-Driving Strategies
JV Recruiting: Joint Ventures Partnerships and Affiliates
Secrets to List Building
Step-by-Step Facebook Marketing: Discover How To Create A Strategy That Will Help You Grow Your Business
Banner Advertising: Traffic Can Be Boosted by Banner Ads
Affiliate Marketing
Improve Your Marketing Strategy with Internet Marketing
Outsourcing Helps You Save Time and Money
Choosing the Right Content and Marketing for Social Media
Make Products That Will Sell
Launching a Product for Affiliate Marketing
Pinterest as a Marketing Tool
Banner Blitz: Mastering the Art of Advertising with Eye-Catching Banners
Beyond Commissions: Maximizing Affiliate Profits with Creative Bonus Strategies
Retargeting Mastery: Winning Sales with Online Strategies
Power Partnerships: Mastering the Art of Business Growth Through Partnership Recruiting
The List Advantage: Unlocking the Power of List Building for Marketing Success
Capital Catalyst: The Essential Guide to Raising Funds for Your Business

Mobile Mastery: The Ultimate Guide to Successful Mobile Marketing Campaigns

Crowdfunding Secrets: A Comprehensive Guide to Successfully Funding Your Next Project

Freelance Freedom: The Essential Guide to Building a Successful Freelance Business

About the Publisher

Accepting manuscripts in the most categories. We love to help people get their words available to the world.

Revival Waves of Glory focus is to provide more options to be published. We do traditional paperbacks, hardcovers, audio books and ebooks all over the world. A traditional royalty-based publisher that offers self-publishing options, Revival Waves provides a very author friendly and transparent publishing process, with President Bill Vincent involved in the full process of your book. Send us your manuscript and we will contact you as soon as possible.

Contact: Bill Vincent at rwgpublishing@yahoo.com

www.ingramcontent.com/pod-product-compliance
Lightning Source LLC
LaVergne TN
LVHW021737060526
838200LV00052B/3324